"Nursing is . . . one of the Fine Arts;
I had almost said, the finest of the Fine Arts."
—Florence Nightingale, *Una and the Lion*, 1868

Henry Holt and Company, LLC
Publishers since 1866
175 Fifth Avenue
New York, New York 10010
mackids.com

Henry Holt® is a registered trademark of Henry Holt and Company, LLC.
Copyright © 2014 by Demi
All rights reserved.

Library of Congress Cataloging-in-Publication Data
Demi.
Florence Nightingale / Demi. – First edition.
pages   cm
Audience: 4-8.
Includes bibliographical references.
ISBN 978-0-8050-9729-0 (hardback)
1. Nightingale, Florence, 1820-1910–Juvenile literature.
2. Nurses–England–Biography–Juvenile literature. I. Title.
RT37.N5D46 2014   610.73092–dc23   [B]   2013030801

Henry Holt books may be purchased for business or promotional use. For information on
bulk purchases, please contact Macmillan Corporate and Premium Sales Department at
(800) 221-7945 x5442 or by e-mail at specialmarkets@macmillan.com.

First Edition—2014
Designed by Ashley Halsey
The artist used watercolor and mixed media to create the illustrations for this book.
Printed in China by South China Printing Co. Ltd., Dongguan City, Guangdong Province

1 3 5 7 9 10 8 6 4 2

Florence Nightingale

DEMI

Henry Holt and Company
New York

Florence Nightingale was born to English parents in Florence, Italy, on May 12, 1820. Just one year earlier, her older sister, Parthenope, had been born in Naples, Italy, which used to be called Parthenope. When Florence was one year old, the Nightingale family returned to England. They lived in a large house called Lea Hurst in Derbyshire.

They were very wealthy, and William Nightingale, Florence's father, had a grand library where he loved to read his books.

Fanny Nightingale, Florence's mother, entertained all the most famous artists, writers, and politicians of the day. For even bigger parties, the Nightingales bought another estate called Embley Park, near London.

Florence didn't like all the parties.
She liked to daydream and play by herself.
She would imagine running a hospital and
made detailed lists and charts of all the
medicine, equipment, and expenses. When
she caught whooping cough, she made a doll
hospital and pretended that her dolls were also
sick. She laid them out with cloths around
their necks in beds set up in a long line, the
way hospitals arranged patients at the time.

When Florence and Parthenope were teenagers, the family traveled throughout Europe. Florence met many famous people and visited beautiful places, but everywhere she went, she noticed the suffering of the sick and the poor people all around her. She kept a detailed record of European hospitals and charities, just like the lists she'd made as a young girl.

Florence was a religious person, and she felt that God wanted her to help people. She soon decided that the way to do this was to become a nurse. But this idea horrified her parents. They wouldn't let her study nursing—they didn't think it was proper for a lady.

In 1847, Florence traveled to Italy with her parents' friends Charles and Selina Bracebridge. Later they went on to Egypt and Germany. While they were in Germany the Bracebridges allowed Florence to visit an orphanage in Kaiserswerth. She spent two weeks there, learning about hygiene and the practice of nursing.

Florence became more convinced than ever that she was meant to be a nurse. Her parents still did not agree, but they eventually saw how determined their daughter was and let her choose her own path.

Florence went to Paris, France, in February 1853, and visited hospitals and poorhouses. She watched doctors and surgeons at work, and she sent questions to hospitals in England, Germany, and France. She took the different answers to these questions and compared them to one another, asking herself which methods were best. These responses helped her teach herself about the world of medicine.

That same year, Florence got her first job, though she wasn't paid for it. She became superintendent of London's Institution for the Care of Sick Gentlewomen in Distressed Circumstances. It was a place where women who were poor and ill could go for medical aid.

Florence made many improvements in her new job. She taught the nurses who worked with her that the hospital must be clean and organized so that they could give the patients the best possible care. She stressed the importance of providing hot water and hot food, and put in bells for the patients to ring when they needed a nurse.

A year later, Florence felt that her work at the
women's hospital was finished. At this time, the
British Army was fighting in the Crimean War, and
reports about the terrible conditions faced by the sick
and injured soldiers were trickling back to England.
Many of the soldiers were suffering from a disease
called cholera. Of course, when Florence heard of
this problem, she began to consider how to fix it.

When she was asked by the Secretary at War
to bring a group of nurses to the military hospital
in Scutari, Turkey, she readily agreed. She knew it
wouldn't be easy, but it was important to her to bring
her medical knowledge and skills to a place where
they were needed.

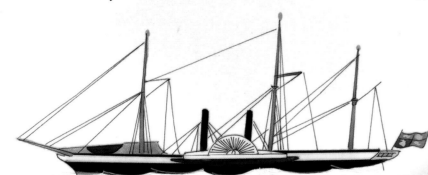

Florence knew that the war hospitals had very few supplies and not enough food. They were usually extremely dirty, without beds for the patients or trained workers who would know how to heal the soldiers.

In Turkey, the doctors were at first reluctant to accept help from Florence and her nurses. But when many more soldiers arrived at the hospital after the Battle of Balaclava, it became clear that help was needed.

Florence arranged for the patients to eat healthy food and worked to get more of the necessary supplies, like bandages and medicines.

Even with these new improvements, though, the soldiers seemed to be staying ill for a long time, and getting sicker rather than better. An investigation soon showed that the sewers weren't draining well. The germs from the sewers were making the soldiers sick. Once this problem was fixed, the patients began to heal.

It was at the military hospital that Florence became known as the Lady with the Lamp. She earned this nickname because she often visited the sick soldiers at night, carrying a small lamp to light her way. The hospital was very dark at night, so it was easy to see Florence, holding her lamp high as she made her rounds.

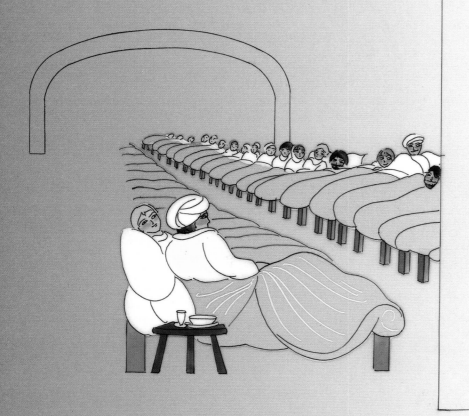

The Crimean War
ended in 1856, and Florence
Nightingale traveled back
to England. She used the
knowledge she had gained
from her experiences during
the war to write reports
about how to make hospitals
better—especially army
hospitals.

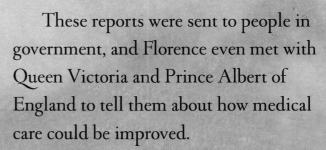

These reports were sent to people in government, and Florence even met with Queen Victoria and Prince Albert of England to tell them about how medical care could be improved.

In 1857, a commission was formed to look into how the British Army took care of wounded and ill soldiers. This commission was a group of people who studied army medical care, and the best resource for this information was Florence Nightingale.

Florence told the men on the commission about her experiences during the Crimean War and explained that improvements like a clean environment and healthy me[a]
would save countless lives.

Her main point was that many [of]
the sicknesses in army hospitals co[uld]
actually be prevented. With better basic care, they could be stopped before they started. This was a new idea, and not everyone was convinced by it.

But Florence kept trying.

Florence worked so hard for other people, fighting to make army hospitals better, that she wore herself out. She collapsed and went to her aunt's house to recuperate. Although she lived many more years, she never truly recovered from this illness.

Florence began to study more than just army medicine. She had identified a serious problem and knew that she must work to make conditions better, not just in one type of hospital but in all hospitals.

Her new goal was to improve the overall organization of hospitals. No detail was too small— she thought about everything from how a hospital should be built so that it was most efficient to how far apart the patients' beds should be.

Florence worked tirelessly to be heard, and it paid off. Many people in England gave money to support her cause. She used this money to set up the Nightingale Fund. It eventually helped to start a school in London, the Nightingale Training School for Nurses, which opened in 1860. The nurses from this school worked all over the world, and they carried Florence's ideas with them.

As time passed, Florence Nightingale's reputation became widely known. In 1861, during the American Civil War, the Union government asked her to share her knowledge about army field medicine. She sent them information, but did not travel to deliver her advice in person.

Florence was once again in poor health. She continued to be an effective and outspoken activist for her causes, but much of the rest of her work was done from bed.

Earlier in her life, Florence had visited several workhouses—institutions set up to house and employ the poor. She had seen the dangerous conditions in such places firsthand and had long been concerned about this issue.

By the mid-1860s, the question of how to care for England's poor was becoming an important one. There were voluntary hospitals, which provided good health care for poor people, but there were many more sick people in the workhouses, which had no trained nurses at all.

Florence was well-known now. She used her contacts in the governme to work toward getting trained nurses into the workhouses and providing goc health care even to those who could no afford to pay for it.

The International Red Cross, which provides medical aid, was begu in 1863. Its founder, Henri Dunant, said that he was inspired by Florence Nightingale's work in the Crimea.

Later, Florence became directly involved with the national branch of the organization, the British Red Cross, when she served as a member of its ladies committee.

Florence continued her work for many more years, writing reports, advocating for improved health care, and sharing her expertise. Although she was ill for much of her life, she lived until the age of ninety. She died peacefully, in her sleep, on August 13, 1910.

She left behind an incredible legacy. The International Red Cross began awarding the Florence Nightingale Medal in 1912, two years after her death. It honors outstanding nurses.

We remember Florence Nightingale today as the driving force behind improvements in nursing during her time and as a woman of extraordinary vision, who believed that no problem, however big it seemed, was ever too big for her to solve.

TIMELINE

MAY 12, 1820: Florence Nightingale is born in Florence, Italy.

1821: The Nightingale family returns to Derbyshire, England.

1847: Florence begins traveling with family friends Charles and Selina Bracebridge and will eventually visit Italy, Egypt, and Germany. In Rome, she meets Sidney and Elizabeth Herbert, who share her passion for improving hospitals.

1850: Florence spends two weeks in an orphanage in Kaiserswerth, Germany, learning about the practice of nursing.

FEBRUARY 1853: Florence visits hospitals and poorhouses in Paris, France, watching how doctors work. She begins to teach herself about the world of medicine.

SPRING 1853: Elizabeth Herbert arranges for Florence to get her fir[st] (unpaid) job as the superintendent of London's Institution for [the] Care of Sick Gentlewomen in Distressed Circumstances. Flor[ence] improves the conditions at the institution, teaching the nurse[s] to keep everything clean and ensuring that the patients have [hot] water, food, and the care and attention they need.

OCTOBER 1853: Britain and its allies become involved in the Crime[an] War against the Russian Empire. Reports about the terrible conditions faced by the sick and injured soldiers and the threa[t of] a disease called cholera start reaching England.

MID-OCTOBER 1854: Florence is asked by Sidney Herbert, who is [the] Secretary at War in the British government, to bring a group o[f] nurses to the military hospital in Scutari, Turkey.

OCTOBER 21, 1854: Florence and 38 nurses set out for Turkey.

OCTOBER 25, 1854: The Russians attack a supply base at Balaclava. [The] British soldiers keep control of the base, but many of them di[e.]

NOVEMBER 1854: Florence and the nurses arrive in Scutari, Turkey, [where] two hospitals for the British Army are located. Although docto[rs at] first refuse to accept help from the women, thousands of casualt[ies] from the continuing battles make them realize they need all the help they can get. Due to her frequent nightly rounds to check o[n the] sick soldiers, Florence becomes known as the Lady with the La[mp.] Despite all her efforts, soldiers continue to die at a high rate.

FEBRUARY 1855: The British government investigates the causes of [the] death at the Scutari hospital. They find that sewer gases from [the] clogged drains are poisoning the patients. Once this cause is [found] and has been dealt with, the death rate drops.

MAY 1855: Florence travels to visit hospitals in the Crimea. While there, she contracts a high fever that prevents her from being able to work again until later that summer.

MARCH 30, 1856: The Treaty of Paris is signed, ending the Crimean War.

JULY 1856: Florence travels back to England and uses her experiences and newfound knowledge to write reports about how to improve medical care and hospitals. She still isn't fully recovered from her earlier fever and writes most of her reports while bedridden.

857: A commission is formed to look into the medical care provided by the British army for wounded and ill soldiers.

860: The Nightingale Training School for Nurses opens in London. Trained nurses will later take Florence's ideas with them when they go to work all over the world.

861: The United States government asks Florence to share her knowledge about army field medicine. Florence sends information, but is still too ill to travel.

863: Inspired by Florence's work, Henri Dunant begins the International Red Cross. Dunant later says of Nightingale, "Though I am known as the founder of the Red Cross and the originator of the Convention of Geneva, it is to an Englishwoman that all the honor of that Convention is due. What inspired me to go to Italy during the war of 1859 was the work of Miss Florence Nightingale in the Crimea."

1907: Florence Nightingale becomes the first woman to be awarded the Order of Merit by King Edward VII of England.

AUGUST 13, 1910: Florence Nightingale dies at 90.

1912: The International Committee of the Red Cross establishes the Florence Nightingale Medal to honor outstanding nurses.

FURTHER READING

Aller, Susan Bivin. *Florence Nightingale*. History Maker Bios. Minneapolis: Lerner Publishing Group, 2007.

Brown, Pam. *Florence Nightingale*. People Who Have Helped the World. Watford, Hertfordshire, UK: Exley Publications Ltd., 1988.

Gorrell, Gena K. *Heart and Soul: The Story of Florence Nightingale*. Plattsburgh, NY: Tundra Books of Northern New York, 2000.

Zemlicka, Shannon. *Florence Nightingale*. On My Own Biography. Minneapolis: Carolrhoda Books, 2003.

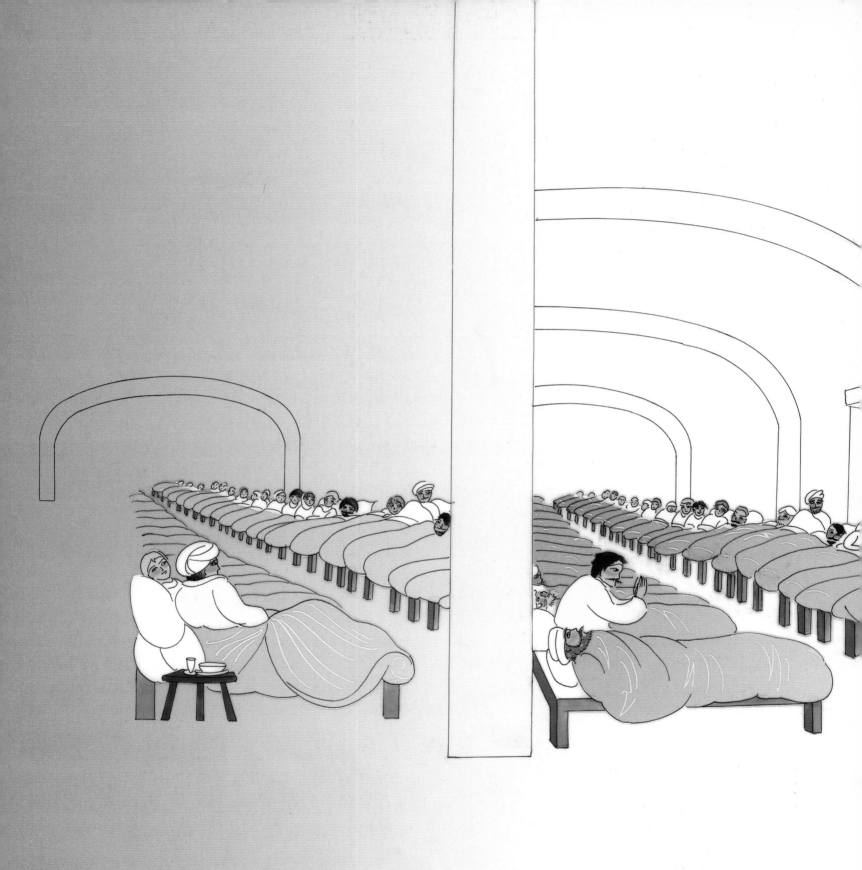